OUR PLACE IN SPACE

Robin Koontz

Rourke
Educational Media

rourkeeducationalmedia.com

Before Reading:

Building Academic Vocabulary and Background Knowledge

Before reading a book, it is important to tap into what your child or students already know about the topic. This will help them develop their vocabulary, increase their reading comprehension, and make connections across the curriculum.

1. *Look at the cover of the book. What will this book be about?*
2. *What do you already know about the topic?*
3. *Let's study the Table of Contents. What will you learn about in the book's chapters?*
4. *What would you like to learn about this topic? Do you think you might learn about it from this book? Why or why not?*
5. *Use a reading journal to write about your knowledge of this topic. Record what you already know about the topic and what you hope to learn about the topic.*
6. *Read the book.*
7. *In your reading journal, record what you learned about the topic and your response to the book.*
8. *After reading the book complete the activities below.*

Content Area Vocabulary

Read the list. What do these words mean?

astrophysicist
catastrophe
cosmos
electromagnetic spectrum
geological
nebula
nuclear fusion
nucleosynthesis
physicists
radiation
reclassification
solar system
spectrometry
sphere
tectonic

After Reading:

Comprehension and Extension Activity

After reading the book, work on the following questions with your child or students in order to check their level of reading comprehension and content mastery.

1. *What causes Earth and other planets to be round?* (Summarize)
2. *What are some reasons people used to think Earth was the center of the universe?* (Infer)
3. *Why is the big bang theory supported by scientists?* (Asking questions)
4. *How can studying rocks help you understand the evolution of the Earth?* (Text to self connection)
5. *Why do you think scientists were punished for proposing theories that did not align with common thinking?* (Asking questions)

Extension Activity

Interested in a career in space? Check out the information on NASA's website www.nasa.gov/audience/forstudents/careers/index.html.
Make a list of opportunities you're interested in pursuing. Then, get started!

Table of Contents

EARLY EARTHLINGS ON A SCARY PLANET

Imagine being one of the first people on Earth. What would you think about the ground under your feet, the sky above? What are those bright objects in the night sky that seem to move and change? And, wow! Why does that huge blinding orb that keeps you warm seem to disappear, only to come back, over and over again?

These natural mysteries outside a human's control were treated in many ways throughout ancient history. Most people thought various gods and goddesses controlled the mysteries around them.

An Astronomical Treasure

The Nebra sky disk is believed to be one of the earliest records of astronomical observation. The 12 inch (30 centimeter) bronze disk was created sometime around 1600 BCE. The 3,600-year-old disk, discovered by amateur treasure hunters in Germany in 1999, features an intricate depiction of the sun, moon, and stars. Native Americans were also drawing what they observed in the sky at about the same time.

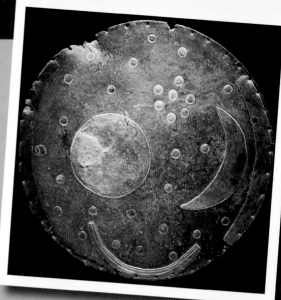

The Nebra sky disk can be seen at the State Museum of Prehistory in Halle, Germany.

In ancient mythology, various gods controlled the oceans. In Greek mythology, Poseidon was king of all the sea gods. The king of the Roman seas was called Neptune. Sumerian myths proclaimed that Amathaunta was the goddess of the oceans.

The sky became the heavens, holding power over their very existence. The oceans and tides were also powerful forces that commanded their respect. The ancient Greeks worshipped Gaea, their word for Mother Earth. They believed that she created the universe.

The ancient peoples told many stories, or myths, describing these and other supernatural beings and their activities. It was their way to explain what was going on in the world around them.

While most people tried to define the unknown as divine beings that ruled over their lives, there were early scientists who wondered about these mysteries in other ways. The earliest recorded scientists who tried to understand the mystery of the heavens were the Babylonians in 1600 BCE. They studied the positions and movements of planets, the moon, and the stars, recording their findings. In the beginning, these scientists suggested that the Earth was flat, or cylindrical, and surrounded by a **cosmos**.

Shaping Our Understanding

Despite scientific evidence that Earth was a sphere, by about 300 CE some early Christians decided this notion was a "pagan absurdity." It wasn't until about a thousand years later that pretty much everyone was convinced that our planet was actually round.

This woodcut from 1475 illustrates the firmament, or sky, that people believed separated the Earth from the heavens, or waters, above it. It is described in the Genesis creation narrative in the Hebrew Bible (Christian Old Testament).

Later, most people believed that Earth was a **sphere** that resided in a spherical universe. The sphere was, after all, the most perfect of all geometric shapes, and the Earth and its cosmos were perfect! But these scientists also observed that a ship would disappear over the horizon and safely return, so a sphere made practical sense as well.

A few hundred years passed before the Greeks used mathematical calculations to figure out that Earth really was a sphere. They were even able to figure out Earth's diameter by using trigonometry.

Blame Gravity!

Why are Earth and other planets round? Gravity pulls toward the center of a planet or star, which pulls everything down into a sphere. But planets and stars are not really perfect spheres. Because they spin, they bulge out a bit around the middle.

Aristotle, a Greek philosopher and scientist from the fourth century BCE, was the first to theorize that our planet was the center of the universe. And Earth was stationary, meaning that it didn't move at all. The sun, moon, planets, and stars moved around it. For almost 2,000 years, Aristotle's theories were considered to be fact. It appeared that the sun and the moon both rose and set. The moon, stars, and planets seemed to move across the night sky. And the ground felt stable, it certainly was not moving. Obviously, planet Earth was a stationary thing and everything in the sky above rotated around it!

Aristotle
384 – 322 BCE

But some scientists questioned these theories. Questioning is a key element in scientific research and discovery. It still took many years, and the invention of the telescope, to finally prove that the Earth was moving, and so were the moon, sun, stars, and other planets. They were all major elements in a shared **solar system**.

As people began to better understand the universe by using science and mathematics, many of the fears and myths were explained and dismissed.

Astronomers finally proved that the planets in our solar system revolve around the sun. They later discovered that our entire solar system takes about 230 million years to orbit around the Milky Way galaxy.

Astronomy, which is the branch of science that studies objects and matter that exist in space and the universe, is probably the first recognized science in human history. Cosmology is a branch of astronomy. The study of cosmology is about the structure and origin of the universe.

Keeping Time

About 30,000 years ago, prehistoric humans kept records of moon phases, possibly as a time-keeping method. The sundial was invented between 5000 and 3500 BCE. It measured the hours in the day as the sun moved across the sky. People also used the heavens to navigate their ships. The sun told them direction, since it always rose in the east and set in the west. At night, the ancient mariners relied on the stars, using their fingers to measure distance and direction based on the position of the stars and planets in the sky.

Build a sundial

You will need:

- scissors
- pencil
- clear tape
- sundial template for your hemisphere, found on this website:

http://d366w3m5tf0813.cloudfront.net/wp-content/uploads/sundial_n.pdf

- your approximate latitude

What you do:

Print the sundial template. You can use the printout or use it to design your own sundial based on the online template. Cut, fold, and tape according to the template's instructions.

STARTING OFF
WITH A BANG?

Our attempts to understand just what our universe is, and where it came from, have sparked a lot of ideas and theories. For instance, from the 15th to the12th Century BCE, some thought that a "cosmic egg" enveloped the sky. This massive egg contained everything in the universe. Many more theories about the origin of the universe were studied and considered.

Then an astronomer named Edwin Hubble proved in 1929 that the universe was expanding. His discovery focused attention on the possibility that perhaps the universe began with a gigantic explosion!

The big bang theory describes the extremely rapid expansion of the universe.

Edwin Hubble
1889-1953

AMAZING ASTROPHYSICIST

Edwin Hubble revolutionized the study of astrophysics. His work at the Mount Wilson Observatory in California led to his discovery of evidence that finally proved that the universe is expanding. He also proved that other galaxies existed in addition to the Milky Way. His classification system for galaxies is called the Hubble sequence. As a tribute to the remarkable astrophysicist, NASA named its Hubble Space Telescope after him.

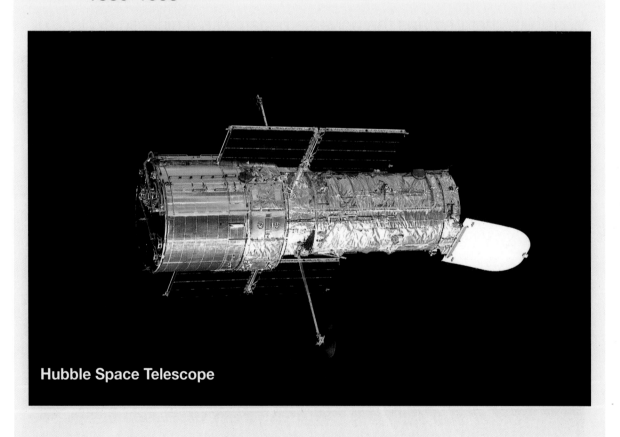

Hubble Space Telescope

This image of the Carina Nebula was taken by the Hubble Space Telescope. The spiraling pillar of dust and hydrogen gas is exposed to radiation from nearby stars, causing the pillar to slowly wear away. Edwin Hubble theorized that nebulae were actually galaxies outside of the Milky Way.

The idea of a big bang was examined by **physicists** and other scientists over the next few years. Though they didn't get much attention for their ideas, more people explored the intriguing idea of this explosive origin of the universe.

In 1948, student Ralph Alpher, along with his PhD professor George Gamov from George Washington University, thought that he had the answers. Thanks to Alpher's mathematical genius and Gamov's previous theories, the men were able to come up with a description of how the universe may have evolved from a big bang.

Their proposal got serious attention. In fact, the *Washington Post* published an April 14, 1948, headline that read, "World Began in 5 Minutes, New Theory."

As more discoveries were made and theories considered, the idea became more credible. Cosmologists even expanded the name to better explain it: big bang **nucleosynthesis**.

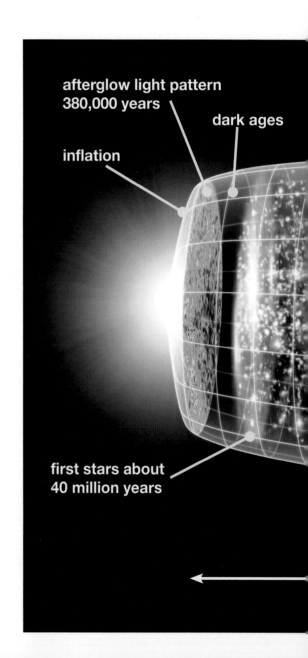

afterglow light pattern
380,000 years

dark ages

inflation

first stars about
40 million years

The idea is difficult to wrap our brains around, and the big bang theory has been questioned and disputed ever since it was first proposed. Was our universe really started by a cosmic **catastrophe** 10 to 20 billion years ago?

Blast From the Past

Astronomers discovered what they believe to be the afterglow of the big bang. Called Cosmic Microwave Background radiation (CMB), the faint glow of light streams through space sort of like the heat that radiates from a rock warmed by the sun. The CMB is the oldest light we have seen so far. It began over 14 billion years ago!

TIMELINE OF THE UNIVERSE
(source: NASA)

development of galaxies, planets, etc.

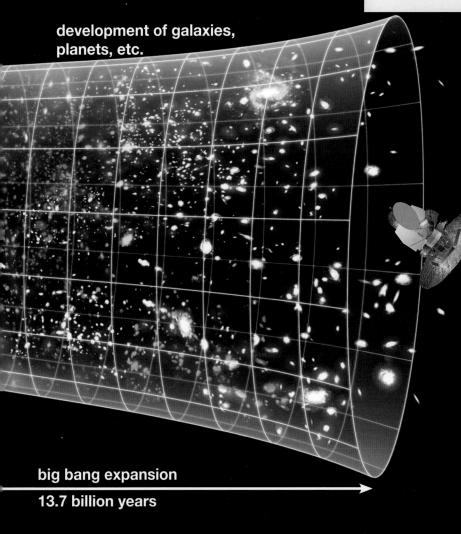

WMAP (Wilkinson Microwave Anisotropy Probe) the spacecraft used to measure the temperature of the cosmic microwave background (CMB) – the radiant heat remaining from the big bang.

big bang expansion

13.7 billion years

Neil DeGrasse Tyson, a famous **astrophysicist**, has defended the big bang theory. Why would an astrophysicist think all the matter, energy, and space of the universe began 15 billion years ago in "a primeval fireball packed into a volume smaller than a marble" that's been continuously expanding since that moment? Because the big bang is supported by a vast amount of evidence and is "the most successful theory ever put forth for the origin and evolution of the universe," he once explained.

Neil DeGrasse Tyson

AMAZING ASTROPHYSICIST

Neil DeGrasse Tyson is an American astrophysicist, teacher, television personality, and author. His love of the universe mostly focuses on stellar evolution, cosmology, galactic astronomy, and stellar formation.

But not everyone agrees, and other theories have been proposed. One idea is referred to as the string theory. Simply put, it proposes that everything is made of very tiny mathematician's string.

In physics, string theory is a theoretical framework in which the point-like particles of particle physics are replaced by one-dimensional objects called strings. String theory describes how these strings spread throughout space and communicate with each other.

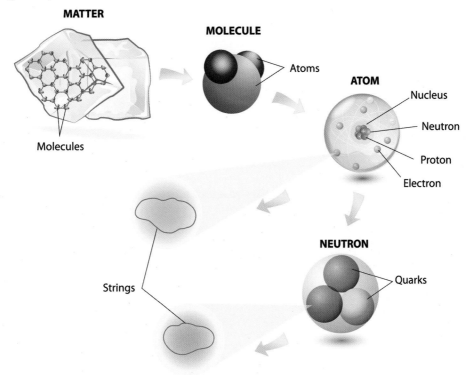

Another idea is that the universe is going through an endless self-sustaining cycle. Some versions of this theory suggest that the universe expands, contracts, and then bounces back. Still another theory is that the universe was born from the death of a previous universe. Even today, astrophysicists and astronomers continue to explore the origins of the universe.

To learn more about objects in the solar system, we use ground based instruments. along with the space based Hubble Telescope.

Astronomers around the globe have been making and recording their findings for hundreds of years. Not only have they made new discoveries, but observed and created thousands of drawings and photographs.

We've learned through these observations that Saturn has rings, Uranus has moons, and Jupiter is made primarily of hydrogen gas. Today even the most basic home telescope can observe the surface of Earth's moon and its many craters.

Uranus

Optical Astronomy

Jupiter

Infrared Astronomy

Saturn

MOTHER EARTH, THE MOON, AND THE SUN

Earth was named more than 1,000 years ago. While all the other planets in the solar system were named after Greek and Roman gods and goddesses, the word Earth just means the ground: eor(th)e and ertha (Old English) and erde (German).

Earth is the fifth largest planet in the solar system and third planet from the sun. Earth's atmosphere protects it, and us, from the airless space above.

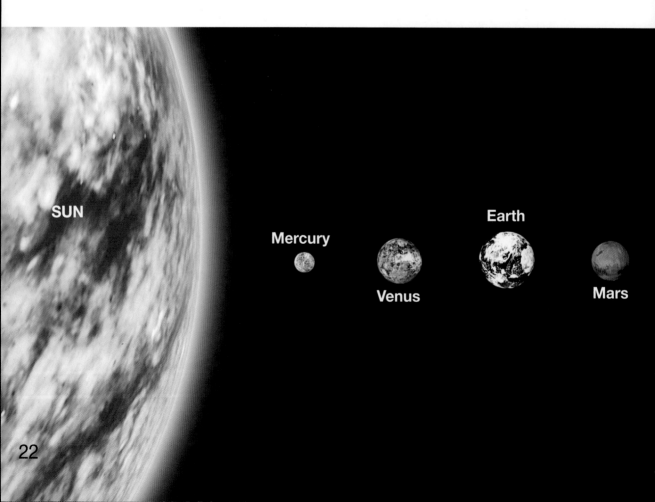

SUN

Mercury

Venus

Earth

Mars

When scientist Galileo Galilei used his mathematical genius to develop the first telescope in 1609, the sky was the limit for many more new discoveries.

Telescopic exploration provided evidence for previous theories. The most important contested theory of the time was that Earth orbited around the sun along with the other planets. Earth was not the center of the universe, as many believed.

Galileo Galilei
1564 - 1642

In 1633, Galileo was found guilty of heresy by the Catholic Church because of his belief that Earth was not the center of the universe. He was sentenced to life under house arrest and died in confinement in 1642.

Jupiter

Uranus

Neptune

Saturn

Sir Isaac Newton, who learned from Galileo, made a lot of important discoveries during his lifetime. But his discovery of the universal law of gravitation helped to explain a lot more about Earth and its solar system. The force of gravity pulls down anything that is not held up by another force, which is why we don't just fly around. Plus, the heavier the object, the greater the gravitational pull.

Sir Isaac Newton
1643 – 1727

Nicolaus Copernicus
1473 – 1543

Center of the Universe

Nicolaus Copernicus was an astronomer and mathematician who lived during the 15th and 16th centuries. He created a concept of a universe where the sun, not Earth, was the center of the universe. This idea was at first extremely controversial, but in time Copernicus was credited with changing the way we viewed the Earth. It helped that Galileo developed the means to prove his theory!

Newton realized that the sun, being the heaviest thing in space, would have the strongest gravitational pull. All the planets, including Earth, move sideways. But the gravity force from the sun holds them so that they orbit around it, rather than just zip off into space.

The Earth also rotates on its axis, counter-clockwise, at a rate of about 1,000 miles per hour (1,600 kilometers per hour). It takes about 24 hours to complete one rotation.

What a Ride!

The Earth travels around the sun along a path that is 600 million miles (970 million kilometers) long. It takes us a year, or 365 days, to make the trip. That means our planet is traveling about 66,000 miles per hour (107,000 kilometers per hour). Can you feel the breeze in your hair?

Scientists study the age of our planet by using the science of geology. Geology is the study of rocks, soil layers, land formations, and other **geological** features to learn about Earth's history.

Volcanoes, **tectonic** shifting, and **erosion** all contribute to Earth's dynamics. Modern dating techniques such as laser heating and a measuring process called mass **spectrometry** help contribute to our knowledge of Earth's age and ancient history. According to geologists, Earth has rotated on its axis day after day, and revolved around the sun, year after year, for about 4.55 billion years.

The Toroweap Point in the Grand Canyon in Arizona was created by wind, rain, and ancient oceans. These forces of nature eroded the soft shale, gypsum, and sandstone over a period of thousands of years. Volcanic activity provided sediment and lava that also sculpted the landforms.

Tectonic plates are sub-layers of Earth's crust. They float, shift, overlap, and sometimes run into each other, often causing earthquakes and volcanic action.

Juan de fuca plate

North American plate

Eurasia plate

Caribbean plate

African plate

Arabia plate

Philippine plate

Cocos plate

Pacific plate

India plate

Pacific plate

South American plate

Nazca plate

Easter plate

Juan Fernandez plate

Australian plate

Scotia plate

Antarctica plate

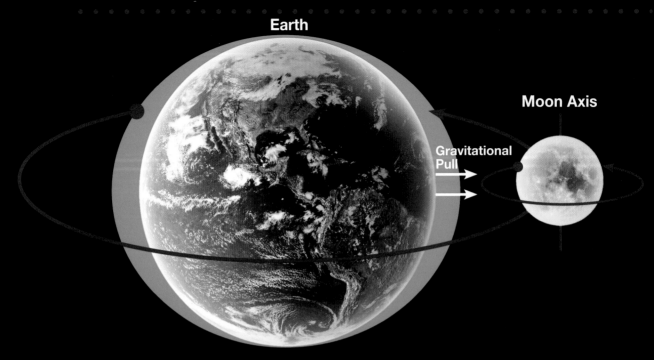

Earth

Moon Axis

Gravitational Pull

The moon, our natural satellite, also rotates on its axis as it orbits Earth. It completes both of its cycles in 27.3 days. The moon phases defined human calendars for thousands of years. They still do in most cultures.

The moon orbits around Earth because of Earth's gravity. Because it rotates as it revolves around Earth, we only see one side of the moon. Its gravity causes regular rises and falls in our sea levels. High tides happen when water bulges upward, and low tides occur when the water drops downward. Many scientists feel that the gravitational pull from the moon is what made Earth a livable planet. It helped to secure a stable climate so that life could flourish.

Every Second Counts!

The gravity of the moon slows down Earth's rotation. About one or two-thousandths of a second are added to our 24-hour day every hundred years. Events such as earthquakes can also change the length of a day. This glitch wasn't noticed until atomic clocks and computers were developed in the 1970s. They keep such accurate time that it became noticeable. So, on rare occasions, an extra second is added to the day, which sometimes wreaks havoc on computer systems around the world.

Lunar Phases

Lunar phases are described as the amount of moon illuminated by the sun, seen from Earth. A fully lit moon is known as the full moon. We describe the moon in phases, using the terms, full, half, and cresent. We then include the terms, waxing, which means expanding, and waning, which means shrinking.

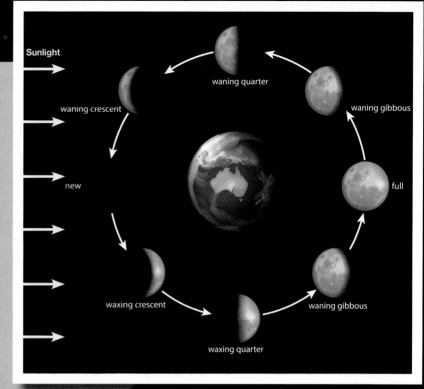

Sunlight

waning quarter

waning gibbous

waning crescent

full

new

waxing crescent

waning gibbous

waxing quarter

Lunar eclipse

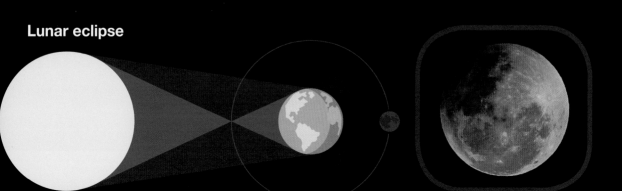

Our primary reason for being alive is the sun. The sun is what holds our solar system together. It is the closest star to Earth, and is filled with extremely hot gases that provide our planet with heat, light, and energy as it drives the seasons, ocean currents, weather, and climate.

The sun doesn't have just one planet orbiting around it year after year. We have seven neighboring planets in our solar system.

WELCOME TO THE NEIGHBORHOOD!

Even before there were telescopes, people could usually tell stars apart from planets. They identified Mercury, Venus, Mars, Jupiter, and Saturn. Named after Roman gods, these planets were originally considered to be wandering stars because they moved relative to the stars. The word planet comes from a Greek word that means wanderer.

The sixth neighbor in our solar system was recognized in 1781. Later named Uranus after the ancient Greek god of the heavens, it wasn't exactly a new discovery. But until then Uranus was considered to be another wandering star.

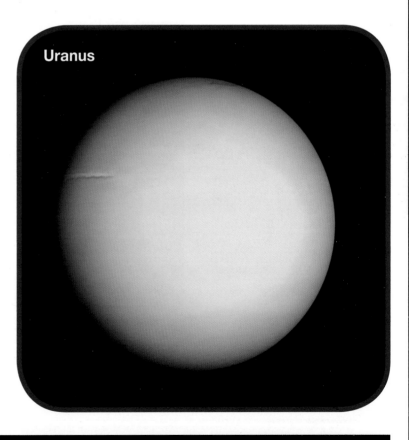

Uranus

Uranus

Neptune, the seventh neighbor, was more of a detective search than a **reclassification** of a star. There appeared to be another planet beyond Uranus because of the way Uranus orbited the sun. A lot of astronomers got involved in the search, and to this day, nobody can agree on who should get the credit. In any case, Neptune was officially discovered in September of 1846. Named after the Roman god of the sea, Earth now had seven neighbors!

The largest member of the neighborhood is Jupiter, then, in order of size, are Saturn, Uranus, Neptune, Earth, Venus, Mars, and Mercury.

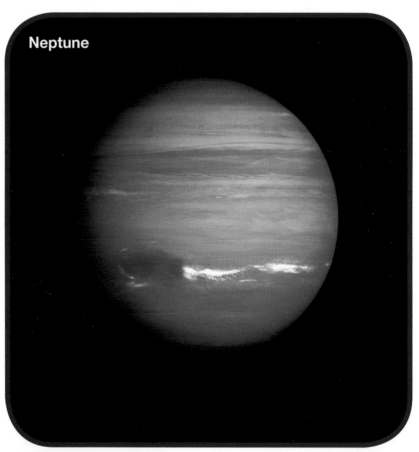

Neptune

Mercury

Venus

Earth

Mars

Jupiter

Saturn

Uranus

Neptune

Four of the planets, including Earth, are terrestrial, or rocky planets. The other rocky planets are Mercury, Venus, and Mars. They are called the inner planets because they are closest to the sun. Terrestrial planets have volcanoes, canyons, craters, and mountains. Earth is the only terrestrial planet in our solar system with liquid oceans. But in recent years it appears that Mars may have once had oceans as well. Both Earth and Mars have polar ice caps.

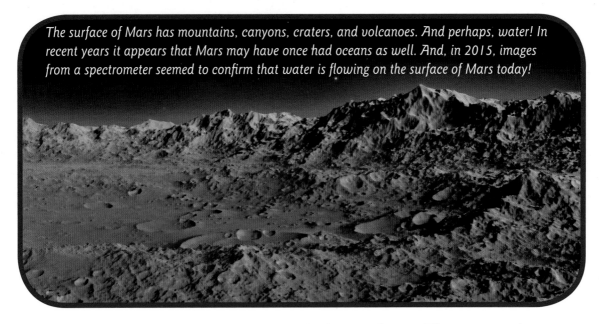

The surface of Mars has mountains, canyons, craters, and volcanoes. And perhaps, water! In recent years it appears that Mars may have once had oceans as well. And, in 2015, images from a spectrometer seemed to confirm that water is flowing on the surface of Mars today!

Our other four neighbors are called gas giants. The outer planets, Jupiter, Saturn, Uranus, and Neptune, are composed mostly of gases such as hydrogen. They also have small amounts of rocky matter, mostly at their cores. All of the gas giants have ring systems, the largest being around Saturn.

Uranus and Neptune are also called "ice giants" because they contain elements that were in ice form when the planets first developed.

Earth's moon

Pluto

Pluto is less than two-thirds of the the size of Earth's moon.

The planet Pluto was discovered in 1930 by astronomer Clyde Tombaugh, and was considered to be the ninth planet in our solar system. Pluto was the farthest planet from the sun and got its name from an 11-year old girl. Pluto was an underworld god and the little girl thought it was a good name because the new planet was so "dark and gloomy."

Pluto was expected to be another gas giant, but instead, it was a small rocky planet smaller than Earth's moon. The new discovery baffled scientists for many years.

Then, in 2003, 73 years after Pluto was discovered, an astronomer named Mike Brown thought he had discovered another new planet, and it was beyond Pluto. Named Eris, the new member of our neighborhood caused other astronomers to reconsider what makes a celestial body a planet. The International Astronomical Union (IAU) talked it over for a few years, and finally made a decision in 2006 that not only affected Eris, but poor Pluto as well. Because both were small and located so far out in the solar system, they were demoted to "dwarf planets."

This artist's depiction of the dwarf planet Eris shows its spherical shape, not the round shape of a classified planet.

Classifying Planets

The IAU's criteria for a new planet was accepted in August, 2006. To be classified as a planet, an object must orbit the sun. It also has to be big enough for gravity to form it into a round-shaped ball. And lastly, it had to clear its orbit, meaning that it had to be big enough to "pull neighboring objects into the planet itself or sling-shot them around the planet and shoot them off into outer space." If an object meets the first two rules for being a planet, then it could be classified as a dwarf planet along with Pluto and Eris. This third criteria is still being debated.

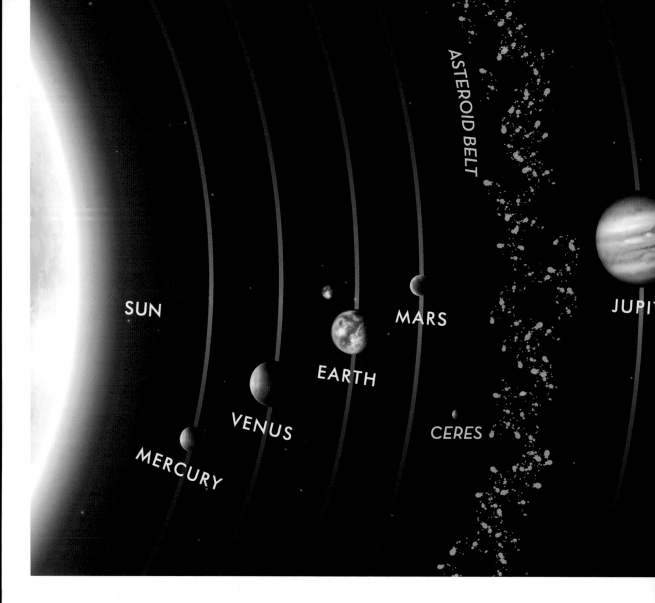

SUN

MERCURY

VENUS

EARTH

MARS

CERES

ASTEROID BELT

JUPI

Pluto's plight is part of how science advances with new knowledge. Scientists now differentiate more than just planets and stars, but everything in between.

Pluto orbits in what is now known as the Kuiper Belt. There are more than 40 other known Kuiper Belt Objects (KBOs) that have been discovered so far and possibly billions yet to be found.

Today, astronomers recognize that all of our neighbors have unique characteristics. As we gain the technology to spy on them

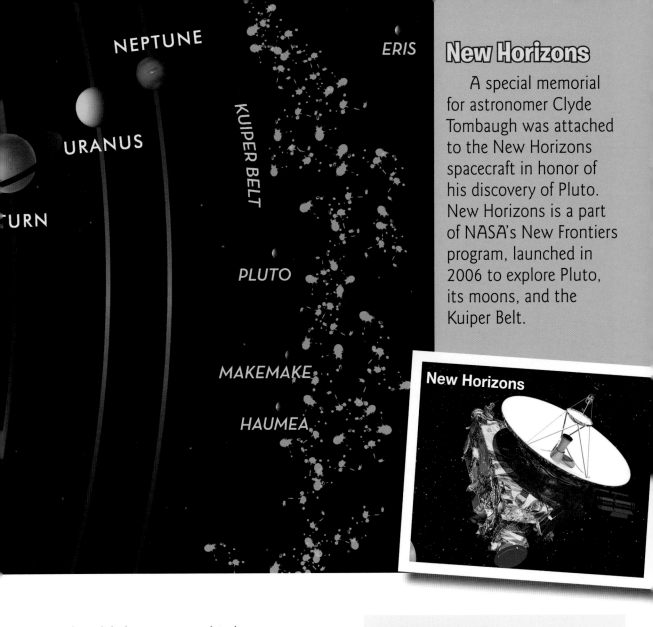

NEPTUNE

ERIS

URANUS

KUIPER BELT

TURN

PLUTO

MAKEMAKE

HAUMEA

New Horizons

A special memorial for astronomer Clyde Tombaugh was attached to the New Horizons spacecraft in honor of his discovery of Pluto. New Horizons is a part of NASA's New Frontiers program, launched in 2006 to explore Pluto, its moons, and the Kuiper Belt.

New Horizons

using high-powered telescopes and spacecraft, we continue to gain more and more information about our solar system. And in recent years, we're learning and discovering more about more distant neighbors many light-years away, in our galaxy called the Milky Way.

Light-Years

Astronomers use the term "light-year" when referring to distance in space, otherwise the numbers would require typing a lot of 0s. One light-year is equal to the distance that light travels in one year (in a vacuum, such as in space). It amounts to about 5.88 trillion miles (9.46 trillion kilometers). For instance, our Milky Way galaxy spans 100,000 light-years from one end to the other.

HOME SWEET HUGE HOME

Our solar system is part of a huge galaxy. A galaxy is basically a system that contains stars, gas, and dust, all held together because of gravitational attraction. A single galaxy can have hundreds of billions of stars in its system.

The Milky Way is our star-packed galaxy. It has a spiral shape with possibly a super-sized black hole in the center. There are millions of clusters of other galaxies strung together throughout the universe. These galaxies come in all sizes, shapes, and colors. The Milky Way is part of one supercluster of galaxies that astronomers named Laniakea.

A Star is Born

Stars are formed from a cloud of gas, called a **nebula**. As nebulae are attracted by gravity, the cloud begins to spin. Atoms bumping into each other make the cloud spin faster, creating heat energy. The cloud gets so hot that **nuclear fusion** happens, making it glow. At this point the cloud is called a protostar. The protostar can continue to grow, becoming a star.

Fasten Your Seatbelts!

Our closest galactic neighbor is called the Andromeda Galaxy. The Milky Way is on a collision course with Andromeda. We are expected to collide in about 5 billion years. At least we have some warning, thanks to science!

Laniakea is a Hawaiian word for "immeasurable heaven," but it is not an accurate description. With the help of a new mapping method for galaxies, astronomers figured out that our super cosmic home is about 520 million light-years in diameter. They used the surrounding galaxies, more than 8,000 in all, to identify the boundaries and determine the measurements.

So if anyone asks where you are on the map, you can tell them your address is: Earth, the solar system, the Milky Way, Laniakea.

Parsecs

Modern astronomers use another unit of distance, called a parsec (pc). One parsec is equal to 3.26 light-years. Really large distances are measured in kiloparsecs (kpc) which are 1,000 parsecs, or megaparsecs (Mpc), which are equal to a million parsecs.

WHO'S OUT THERE?

Our humble address in the universe is a reminder of how much we don't know about what, or who, is out there in space. Astronomers are always on the lookout for any Earth-like planet that might support life, or could have supported life in the past.

There are several conditions a planet needs in order to support life as we know it. The planet needs to be in a habitable zone, meaning that it's not too hot, not too cold, has water and light, is a terrestrial planet, and it must be protected from **radiation** and other potential life killers. Also, to grow and sustain living organisms, the planet needs to have oxygen and nitrogen.

Planetary Exploration

At Kennedy Space Center in Florida, NASA is developing drones called Extreme Access Flyers. These robots will be able to survive the inhospitable conditions in space as they search for and gather samples from other worlds.

Right now, astrobiologists, people who study the possibility of life beyond Earth, believe that the Milky Way alone may have 500 habitable planets. Given that the Milky Way is only one of billions of galaxies in the universe, the possibilities of other life in the universe seems possible. All we have to do is look for it!

The 21st century began with what many in the field declared was the golden age of astronomy. There are hundreds of space-based, airborne, ground- and underground-based astronomical observatories at work around the globe, and many more in the planning or near-launch stages.

Is There Life Out There?

Astrobiologists have expertise in various sciences such as astronomy, biological sciences, and geophysics. They study the different moons and planets and the information gathered about them, trying to determine if the right conditions exist, or existed in the past, to support life. They often conduct their studies by exploring extreme life and life's origins here on Earth. Some search for radio signals from intelligent life in the universe. Whatever their methods of research and study, their goals are the same, to answer three questions: How does life begin and evolve? Does life exist elsewhere in the universe? What is the future of life on Earth and beyond?

Meanwhile, advanced new technology has allowed astronomers to be able to observe the entire **electromagnetic spectrum**. This makes it possible to unlock even more mysteries of the universe. These days, astronomers rarely need to actually look through the eyepiece of a telescope. Technology has brought them instruments of observation that are nothing like Galileo or anyone else who began it all could imagine in their wildest dreams.

Activity

Build Your Own Hubble Telescope
Want to impress your teacher? Build a scale model of the Hubble Telescope. NASA's HubbleSite has instructions for a few models. Check it out!

http://hubblesite.org/the_telescope/hand-held_hubble

Mars Rovers

The Mars Rovers behave like mechanical geologists on the surface of the Red Planet, otherwise known as Mars. They use robotic senses to gather and record information for scientists back on Earth as they rove around on their legs and wheels.

Kepler 186f

For instance, Kepler 186f, discovered in 2014, was the first planet in the Milky Way that was validated to be an Earth-size planet in a habitable zone. It is about 500 light-years from Earth. There are four companion planets which all orbit around a red star that is about half the size and mass of Earth's sun. The distant system was discovered using NASA's Kepler Space Telescope. Both current and future NASA missions hope to learn more about this and other Earth-like planets.

NASA's first human space flights were part of the Apollo Program. After Apollo, NASA's Space Shuttle program provided 30 years of amazing achievements in the U.S. space program. The International Space Station, a partnership that represents 15 nations, has enabled people to learn about how to both work and live in space for months at a time.

What's Making that Star Wobble?

In 2009, the Automated Planet Finder (APF) at Lick Observatory in California discovered a wobble in the star HD 7924. Astronomers knew that a wobble was usually caused by gravitational pull of planets that were orbiting around it. They first discovered one planet, but they kept looking, using specialized instruments and software. In 2015, they found two more planets also orbiting HD 7924.

The Automatic Photometric Telescope (APT) at Fairborn Observatory in Arizona also helped with the discovery. The new-found planets are called "super-earths" because they are larger than Earth but smaller than Neptune.

The APF at the Lick Observatory was the first telescope able to detect rocky planets in other solar systems that might support life. Also called RPF (Rocky Planet Finder), the extrasolar planet hunter operates robotically.

After 50 years of space research, NASA is working on the next exciting chapters of exploration. Soon, space transportation will be available through private and commercial sectors. There are already plans to develop space vehicles that are reliable, safe, and cost-effective for transporting cargo, crew, and even passengers. NASA is also developing the means for humans to soar into deep space exploration. Technically advanced systems will take astronauts to places no one has gone before, including Mars.

This golden age and the projected future of astronomy and astrophysics make the field a very exciting time to be an astronomer. Discoveries are made nearly every second, and the sky, as we now know, is not the limit. It is limitless.

Eyes to the Skies

Ready to do some stargazing? The smallest telescope or even high-powered binoculars can spot these five celestial objects on a clear night:

Orion Nebula

Andromeda Galaxy

Hercules Globular Cluster

Crab Nebula

Whirlpool Galaxy

Warp Speed!

Albert Einstein's theory of relativity states that nothing can surpass the speed of light. But an astrophysicist named Geraint Lewis from the University of Sydney in Australia feels that perhaps traveling faster than the speed of light is possible; the challenge is simply finding the right materials to be able to do it. That material just needs to have "negative density energy." That means it would be able to warp space so that it twists itself around a spacecraft. While currently nobody has figured out how to do that, considering how far astrophysics has come in just a couple hundred years, who knows what the future will bring?

GLOSSARY

astrophysicist (ass-truh-FIZ-uh-sist): a scientist who studies stars, planets, and other objects in the universe

catastrophe (kuh-TASS-truh-fee): a terrible and sudden disaster

cosmos (KOZ-muhss): the universe

electromagnetic spectrum (i-LEK-troh-mag-nit-ik SPEK-truhm): the entire range of wavelengths or frequencies of electromagnetic radiation that includes visible light

geological (gee-oh-LOJ-ik-uhl): referring to the science that studies rocks, layers of soil, and other natural formations to learn about the history of Earth and its life

nebula (NEB-yuh-luh): a bright, cloudlike mass that can be seen in the night sky

nuclear fusion (NOO-klee-ur FYOO-zhuhn): a nuclear reaction in which two or more atomic nuclei come very close and then collide at a very high speed and join to form a new type of atomic nucleus

nucleosynthesis (nu-klee-oh-SIN-thuh-siss): the production of a chemical element from simpler nuclei (as of hydrogen) especially in a star

physicists (fiz-uh-sists): scientists who study physics

radiation (RAY-dee-AY-shun): particles sent out by a radioactive substance

reclassification (re-klass-uh-fuh-kay-shuhn): changing the class of something

solar system (SOH-lur SISS-tuhm): the collection of eight planets and their moons in orbit around the sun, together with smaller bodies in the form of asteroids, meteoroids, and comets

spectrometry (spek-TROM-uh-tree): an instrument used for measuring wavelengths of the light spectrum

sphere (sfihr): a solid shape like a basketball or globe, with all points of the shape the same distance from the center of the shape

tectonic (tek-TON-ik): relating to changes in the structure of Earth's surface

INDEX

SHOW WHAT YOU KNOW

1. Why did Aristotle's belief that Earth was the center of the universe make so much sense?
2. Why were the first five planets in our solar system the easiest to identify?
3. What invention changed the course of astronomy?
4. What must a planet have in order to support life, as we know it?
5. What are three things that the force of gravity affects in the universe?

WEBSITES TO VISIT

www.spaceplace.nasa.gov
www.skyandtelescope.com
www.nasa.gov

ABOUT THE AUTHOR

Robin Koontz is a freelance author/illustrator/ designer of a wide variety of nonfiction and fiction books, educational blogs, and magazine articles for children and young adults. Her 2011 science title, *Leaps and Creeps - How Animals Move to Survive*, was an Animal Behavior Society Outstanding Children's Book Award Finalist. Raised in Maryland and Alabama, Robin now lives with her husband in the Coast Range of western Oregon where she especially enjoys observing the wildlife on her property. You can learn more on her blog: robinkoontz.wordpress.com.

Meet The Author!
www.meetREMauthors.com

www.rourkeeducationalmedia.com

PHOTO CREDITS: Cover and title page: milky way background © Stefano Garau, Earth © MarcelClemens, Earth's Moon © NOAA, grid background © fluidworkshop; page 4-5 © Valeri Potapova, page 5 inset © Dbachmann; page 6-7 © Shane Myers Photography, page 8 © MarcelClemens; page 10-11 © fluidworkshop, page 12 © venation, page 13 © Igor Zh.; pages 14, 15 and 17 courtesy of NASA; page 18 © Napolean_70, page 19 © Designua; page 20-21© NASA/JPL-Caltech; page 22-23, 31, 32 © Bobboz; page 25 © cigdem; page 26-27 © sumikophoto; page 27 map © Designua; page 28-29 © Aphelleon; page 30 © Aphelleon, page 31 and 32 main photo © Tristan3D, page 33 © HelenField; page 34 moon © dzika_mrowka, Pluto © Vadim Sadovski; page 35 © ESO/L. Calçada and Nick Risinger (skysurvey.org); page 36-37 © fluidworkshop, page 37 inset photo of New Horizons © NASA/ Johns Hopkins University Applied Physics Laboratory/Southwest Research Institute; page 38-39 © http://www.eso.org/public/images/milkyway/; page 40 © NASA/Swamp Works; page 42 top © Designua, bottom © NASA/JPL-Caltech/MSSS, page 43 courtesy of NASA Ames/SETI Institute/JPL-Caltech; page 44 © Oleg Alexandrov, page 45 Orion Nebula courtesy of NASA, ESA, M. Robberto (Space Telescope Science Institute/ESA) and the Hubble Space Telescope Orion Treasury Project Team, Andromeda courtesy NASA/JPL-Caltech/UCLA, Hercules Globular Cluster © Rawastrodata, Crab Nebula courtesy NASA, ESA, J. Hester and A. Loll (Arizona State University), Whirlpool Galaxy courtesy NASA and European Space Agency

Edited by: Keli Sipperley

Cover and Interior design by: Nicola Stratford   www.nicolastratford.com

Library of Congress PCN Data

Our Place in Space / Robin Koontz
(Let's Explore Science)
ISBN 978-1-68191-390-2 (hard cover)
ISBN 978-1-68191-432-9 (soft cover)
ISBN 978-1-68191-471-8 (e-Book)
Library of Congress Control Number: 2015951557

Also Available as:

ROURKE'S
e-Books

Printed in the United States of America, North Mankato, Minnesota